HEREFORD
IN OLD PHOTOGRAPHS

HIGH STREET in c. 1900.

HEREFORD
IN OLD PHOTOGRAPHS

COLLECTED BY
ANNE SANDFORD

ALAN SUTTON
1987

Alan Sutton Publishing Limited
Brunswick Road · Gloucester

First published 1987

British Library Cataloguing in Publication Data

Hereford in old photographs.
1. Hereford (Hereford and Worcester) ——
Social life and customs —— Pictorial works
I. Sandford, Anne
942.4'46081'0222   DA690.H54

ISBN 0–86299–414–4

For Alice

Cover: HEREFORD HIGH TOWN c. 1897

**Typesetting and origination by
Alan Sutton Publishing Limited
Printed in Great Britain
by WBC Print Ltd · Bristol**

CONTENTS

INTRODUCTION   7

1.   STREETS AND LANDMARKS   9

2.   SHOPS AND PUBS   39

3.   PEOPLE, PLACES AND WORK   59

4.   HIGHDAYS AND HOLIDAYS   85

5.   DISASTER, FIRE AND FLOOD   111

6.   RECREATION   121

7.   TRANSPORT   145

     ACKNOWLEDGEMENTS   159

THE CATHEDRAL AND CASTLE CLIFFE from the river in 1892. The buildings on the right were, for many years, Hereford College of Art. Before that they were the eighteenth-century meeting place and coffee house of The Society of Tempers, dedicated to 'communal well being'.

INTRODUCTION

This collection of photographs ranges in date from 1859 to the 1960s, and reflects the subjects considered to be of interest to photographers, both professional and amateur, in those times. Many facets of society in this cathedral city have been captured on film for posterity, some of the most revealing being those depicting the people disporting themselves, or posing proudly with the tools of their trade. Numerous photographs exist of the River Wye, the cathedral and heart of the city and it has been a most rewarding task to select new and interesting views of its perennial beauty and attractions. Great events such as royal visits and the historic Three Choirs Festival are well represented, but some of the most fascinating photographs reflect the changes in the urban landscape over the last hundred years. Photography is perhaps the most telling historical record we have.

We are fortunate that many negatives and prints produced by the antiquarian and pioneer photographer, Alfred Watkins (of *The Old Straight Track* fame), remain in the City Library, as well as the painstaking records of F.C. Morgan taken in the 1920s and 1930s. The work of professional photographers W.H. Bustin of Palace Yard, Preece, Wilson, Ladmore, and Unwin, together with many others, is still available at the County Record Office and City Museum collections. However, although much work by some photographers of the period has disappeared, there always remains the possibility and hope that this will, at some time, be discovered; probably in the most unexpected and unlikely places! Fortunately, wonderful pictures are to be found in family albums, many of which can now be seen in this collection for the first time.

I trust that this modest compilation of photographs of our city and its activities of former years, will provide as much pleasure to you as its research and assembly has to me.

THE OLD HOUSE stands proudly in High Town, in its days as a bank in the 1920s — the last remaining sentinel of Butchers' Row, guarded by a member of the local constabulary! Roberts & Sons' fine bakery van was a favourite sight in the city.

Streets
and Landmarks

A PHOTOGRAPH OF THE RIVER WYE from the Cathedral Tower, c. 1910.

WHITECROSS, HEREFORD, in 1891. A family take a well-earned rest on a Sunday stroll, perhaps unaware that it was the site of a plague market in 1361. Money for country produce was left on the steps by the beleagured citizens of the City of Hereford.

GASLIT HIGH TOWN on a snowy night in 1897. The cab ranks were full, but many of the 'cabbies' were possibly huddled around the brazier in the central 'cabbies' hut. The hut can still be found in use as an office for the tennis courts on the Bishop's Meadow.

VIEW OF GWYNNE STREET C. 1859. The house on the left is reputed to have been the birthplace of Nell Gwynne. The houses in Pipewell Lane were demolished shortly after this photograph was taken.

FELLING THE ELMS in the Cathedral Close in the freezing conditions of February 1916. Women are stripping the branches and preparing the logs to take home to their families.

ALL SAINTS CHURCH c. 1900; note the savage railings placed to stop vagrants or thieves with nefarious intent sheltering beside the church. It is interesting also to see the fine house to the left of the church before the doorway was lost to shop conversion.

HEREFORD IS VERY FORTUNATE IN HAVING A SECOND CHAINED LIBRARY, containing 326 books, in All Saints Church. It is the second largest chained library in the country. We are lucky to have these books as they were sold in the last century for £100 by an unscrupulous churchwarden. Luckily the Dean of Windsor and the Bishop were able to prevent their removal to America and they were returned to their rightful 'home' where they can be seen today.

THE CHAINED LIBRARY, one of the Cathedral's greatest treasures, contains around 1,444 volumes dating back to the Anglo-Saxon period. The library can be visited by the public and is housed in the upper transept and upper cloister rooms.

AN EARLY POSTCARD OF THE CHAINED LIBRARY in Hereford Cathedral; the largest chained library in England.

AN IVY-COVERED CITY WALL BASTION beside Greyfriars House, St Nicholas Street, before the ring road.

KING STREET AND THE CORNER OF AUBREY STREET in October 1958. A wonderful collection of buildings have disappeared here including the fine 'Residence' on the corner.

ST MARTINS STREET, c. 1900. The fine collection of posters reflects many aspects of Hereford life, with adverts for cycles, overcoats and even the famous Wye boot for 4s.11d.

CLEARING OF THE GAOL SITE, Commercial Road, in 1935, to make way for the bus station. Note the Fowler traction engine on the right.

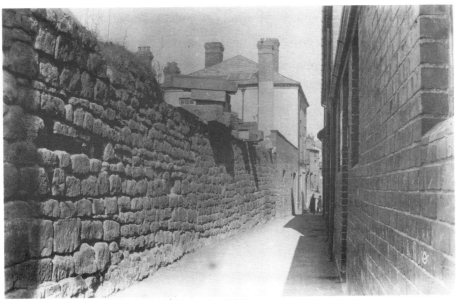

THE MEDIEVAL CITY WALL at Gunners Lane in 1926.

A FINE HALF-TIMBERED HOUSE in Little Berrington Street, demolished in January 1938 and recorded by Basil Butcher.

THE TELEPHONE EXCHANGE, under construction behind Church Street in 1949.

THE NEW ROLLER-SKATING RINK, under construction at the end of Bewell Street in 1909. It measured 114ft. by 65ft. The architect was Mr Herbert Skyrme of Widemarsh Street and the contractors were Messrs Wilks & Son of Whitecross Road, Hereford. This rink was popular but shortlived, rather like the recent skate-boarding craze, although roller-skating is now undergoing a revival. Any further details on the rink would be most gratefully received by the Museum.

BROAD STREET, C. 1904, looking westwards. Showing the Green Dragon Hotel and beyond, the Corn Exchange which later became the Kemble Theatre (1912); now alas, demolished for a modern (1960s) office block.

THE GREEN DRAGON, Hereford's best-known hotel, in C. 1905. It is interesting to see the original coaching entrance on the right; the coach house and stables were at the rear of the hotel and are now the hotel garage. The hotel's frontage, as seen here, was built in 1857 together with the assembly room and ballrooms.

THE OAK SITTING ROOM in the Green Dragon Hotel, photographed by Alfred Watkins in 1932. This panelled Jacobean room has a wonderful ribbed plaster ceiling and an earlier fifteenth-century frieze set into the fireplace. This room was found when two houses were demolished for the 1931–2 hotel enlargement and re-construction.

THE SPLENDID HALF-TIMBERED MARCHANTS' BUILDING IN HIGH TOWN, sadly exposed awaiting its removal during the building of Littlewoods Store in the 1960s. The building was once an apothecary's shop and there are stories of a ghostly apothecary, who accidently killed his assistant, staring poignantly out of the top window on cold winter nights.

THE SHELL OF MARCHANTS' stands in High Town near the Old House awaiting its ignominious re-location to the Littlewoods building. Many people remember the building in High Town during the 1960s and believe that the Old House was the building that was moved. Luckily the Old House remains in its original position, the last remaining house of Butcher's Row. Thousands walk and drive past Marchants' today in its demoted position, failing to notice one of the most interesting half-timbered buildings in the city.

ALFRED WATKINS' POSTCARD OF THE HALL IN THE OLD HOUSE was taken c. 1929 when the Old House Committee had begun to create the Museum with suitable loans and purchases. Note the left-hand wall by the settle, before the stairs were moved to this location.

THE HALL AND STAIRCASE in the Old House much as it is today.

THE OLD HOUSE in its hey-day as a bank in the late 1920s. Originally the Worcester City & County Bank and later Lloyds Bank, it was generously presented to the city by Lloyds in 1928, when it became one of the City Museums. It is now a key tourist attraction.

HENRY BETTINGTON'S RARE PHOTOGRAPH OF THE NORTH SIDE OF COMMERCIAL STREET, in 1914, before the building of Wilson's Chambers. In this street one could find a hatter, tailor, hairdresser, clothier, Lindsey-Price house furnishers, a grocer, ironmonger, butcher, newsagent and tobacconist.

AN UNUSUAL VIEW OF THE CORNER OF WIDEMARSH STREET and Maylord Street in the 1920s, before the building of the Electricity Showrooms as we know it today.

FRYER'S GARAGE, Widemarsh Street, in 1961. Note the two substantial cottages on the left of the photograph. The car parked on the road was offered for sale at £165 and you could purchase a car for £2 12s.6d. by weekly instalments!

HENLY'S GARAGE, formerly Fryer's, in c. 1964. The two cottages in the previous photograph were demolished to extend the showrooms. Now Henly's, in its turn, has been demolished.

ST GILES HOSPITAL CHAPEL (built in 1672) on the corner of Ledbury Road and St Owen's Street in 1926, before the road improvements, when it was removed and rebuilt in its present position. It led a charmed life once the motor vehicle became popular — several lorries had near misses!

ST GILES CHAPEL, Ledbury Road, 1926.

AN EXCITING DISCOVERY IN 1927 on the corner of Ledbury Road and St Owens Street, when the foundations of the mid twelfth-century Knights Templar's Round Chapel were uncovered underneath the seventeenth-century Chapel of St Giles. St Giles Chapel was removed stone by stone and re-erected. A plaque recording the Templar Chapel and some stones can be found just behind the bench on the corner of Ledbury Road, passed by Herefordians every day, unaware of this piece of history beneath their feet.

ST PETER'S SQUARE taken on 13 December 1935 at 11.30p.m. with three 2,000c.p.(candle power) HP Keith lamps.

THE OTHER END OF COMMERCIAL STREET taken at the same time of night in 1934. Cope's fine shop front on the right shows 'K' shoes selling well. Everyone seems to have been tucked up in bed by 11.30p.m.!

COMMERCIAL STREET AT NIGHT in March 1934, lit by Keith 1,000c.p. HP lamps. Chadd's Department Store, on the left, is still there today, but the Trinity Almshouses on the right are no more.

COMMERCIAL SQUARE AT 11.35p.m. in January 1935. Note the buildings on the left, including the famous Black & White Fish & Chip Saloon, now long gone (ring road) – the new lamps made the street reminiscent of a French boulevard!

A POSTCARD OF THE GENERAL HOSPITAL, Nelson Street, with the new verandah; note the young patients wheeled out in their beds to enjoy the fresh air and the peaceful view of the River Wye.

BREINTON AVENUE, off Westfaling Street, under construction. The cemetery can be seen on the left of the photograph.

THE BUILDING OF THE 'GARDEN CITY' in 1909. Each semi-detached 'cottage' contained, 'on ground floor, small hall, parlour, living room, kitchen, larder, coal-store and WC and on first floor, three bedrooms and bathroom (with hot and cold water). Rent, including rates and taxes, 7s. 9d. each' The development was opened by the Mayoress, Mrs E.F. Bulmer.

A SIMILAR DEVELOPMENT AT EIGN MILL ROAD during the First World War, not long after completion. A lone Boy Scout, with military escort, poses proudly!

THE BUILDING OF GODWIN'S VICTORIA TILE WORKS, beside the Hereford and Gloucester Canal, College Road, in 1884.

HIGH TOWN, c. 1900, shows a famous Hereford sight to the left – Mr Panicalli's Ice Cream cart. The young lad appears to be sampling his wares! The coach is very like the Judge's Coach, now restored and at Churchill Gardens Museum. The Judge's lodgings on the left are next door to Kings, and Augustus Edwards' fine Emporium has a delightful display of winter coats. The gentleman outside the shop, with the bag, is possibly a commercial traveller of the day.

ST PETER'S STREET AND HIGH TOWN in 1904. Produced by Wilson & Phillips at the Post Office, Eign Street, this interesting postcard shows an early car on the left, Coles the drapers, The Elephant & Castle, Lennards Ltd., Boots, Davies & Son – dyers, Hatton & Bros and Roberts & Sons – bakers. The Old House Bank in the centre looks as if banking had not yet commenced for the day!

A PEACEFUL VIEW OF THE CASTLE POOL from the Cantilupe Gardens, c. 1925.

SECTION TWO

Shops and Pubs

THE FASCINATING FRONTAGE OF HARDING BROTHERS, Commercial Street, was demolished in 1964 to make way for Tescos, which in turn has become McDonalds and the Early Learning Centre.

DR BREWSTER'S FINE MANSION HOUSE, Widemarsh Street, built in 1697 as a private house and photographed in January 1907. In 1900 the building was used for municipal purposes, containing offices of the City Surveyor, Rate Collectors and the Gas & Waterworks Department.

THE MANSION HOUSE after its conversion into shops, July 1907.

THE NEW MARKS & SPENCERS PENNY BAZAAR & STORES well underway in High Street – eagerly awaited by the population of Hereford. The heavy shoring next door must have been quite a traffic hazard.

DEMOLITION IN JUNE 1928, to allow the building of the original Marks & Spencers in High Town. Marchants can be seen through the site on the other side of the road.

BUSINESS AS USUAL FOR MASTERS & CO. outfitters, in spite of the shoring by Marks & Spencers. The summer stock of Panama hats is well to the fore. Now part of Boots in High Street, this shop was renowned throughout the 1920s and 30s for reasonably priced clothing.

A FINE SALE AT RATHBONES', the Carlton Shoe Shop, gives us a glimpse of high fashion in Hereford in 1928. What splendid shoes and cloche hats, all at reduced prices owing to the building of Marks along the street!

A WONDERFUL SIGN ON THE CARLTON SHOE CO. PREMISES exhorts Herefordians to 'buy your shoes here in safety'! A fine selection of shoes for the 20s flapper and of course the more matronly client.

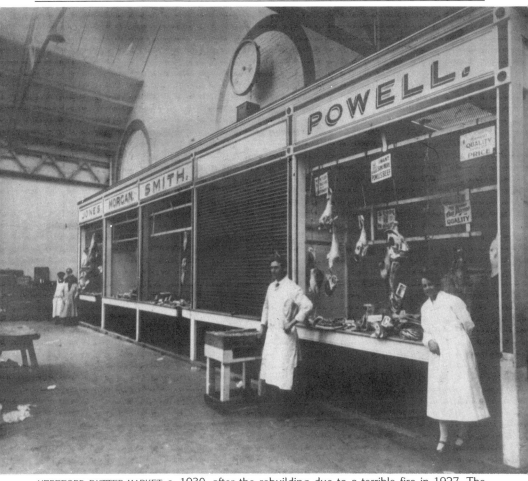

HEREFORD BUTTER MARKET C. 1930, after the rebuilding due to a terrible fire in 1927. The butchery part of the market was much patronised by Herefordians and country people, particularly on a Wednesday – market day. Powell's stall was in operation until about 28 years ago.

PRITCHARD & SONS, Tailors of High Town, during the First World War. In the left-hand window, everything for the well-equipped young Army Officer is on view.

A CLOSE-UP VIEW OF MATTHEW OATFIELD'S IRONMONGERS SHOP in the Old House c. 1879. Fletcher's wet fish shop can just be seen on the right of this photograph. Note the wonderful range of baskets, pots and pans. Times change, the type of objects outside are now Museum specimens *inside* the City Museum!

THE ORANGE TREE and Ladmore's fine Radio & Cycle Shop in 1939. Note that Nelson Eddy was on at the Ritz in *Let Freedom Ring*.

KING STREET after the demolition of Ladmore's Cycle Shop, c. 1958, in order to build Assurance Offices.

THE SEVENTEENTH-CENTURY BLACK LION HOTEL, Bridge Street, showing the interesting discovery of the half-timbered structure in the summer of 1909. New plasterwork was applied and the timbers were carefully hidden and only re-exposed in the 1970s. In the 1930s, wonderful early wall paintings depicting the Ten Commandments were discovered. Sadly they are not on public view.

THE WHALEBONE INN, Old Eign Hill from a stereoscopic photograph. Formerly a public house serving the Eign Wharf, it possessed fine whalebones which were displayed in the entrance, giving the inn its unusual name. The pub is no more; now a veterinary surgery stands on the site, but where are the whalebones? Any information will be gratefully received.

THE RAILWAY INN, Barton Road, in the 1940s – now the 'Antelope Inn'. It was well frequented by railwaymen from Barton Station.

THE BARTON TAVERN in the 1940s, demolished in the 1960s to make way for the ring road. At the turn of the century, the Tavern was the popular haunt for the workers at Barton Tannery in Barton Road.

A POSTERN GATE in the city wall during the rebuilding of the Wellington Inn at the corner of Widemarsh Street in the 1890s.

G.H. GODSELL'S IMPERIAL HOTEL, Widemarsh Street, and the Raven Hotel on the corner of Maylord Street, c. 1950. The Imperial is not changed, but the 'Raven' is no more.

A GROUP OUTSIDE THE CITY AND COUNTY DINING ROOMS, Commercial Street, later the 'Tabard'. The gentlemen and boys are all wearing unusual buttonholes. If anyone recognises this intriguing insignia, the people or the place, I would be delighted to hear from them. This postcard was sent to Miss Gardner at 17 Bath Street, in August 1905, signed 'With love, the Old Boys'.

THE MEDIEVAL BOOTH HALL, with its fine hammer beam and arch-braced collar-beam roof. It was at one time the Hall of Mercer's Guild, with bolts of Welsh cloth laid out in profusion below the carved angels. Later it became an inn, as it is today, but no inebriated customer would have wished to cross Tom Spring, landlord in the 1830s and former boxing champion of all England!

HERBERT HATTON AND HIS SON JOHN in the renowned Hatton Fishing Tackle Shop, St Owen Street, in the 1950s.

THE NEW HARP IN UNION STREET in the 1920s, showing the 'chequers' sign. These rare metal panels are now in the Museum collection. They are alternate diamonds or lozenges of green and red. The 'chequers' originated as the counting board used in the medieval period for counting money. It was adopted by innkeepers as a sign that they kept a counting board for the use of customers. 20 silver pennies = 1 ounce, when placed on each square, each row of 8 made 'a mark', one and a half rows made 'a pound'. A similar sign was found near the Booth Hall.

People, Places and Work

R.P.RAVENHILL. H.MINTON. S.W.POWELL.   J.WALL.   A.R.GROOM. E.WILLIAMS.

THE FAMOUS HEREFORDSHIRE PLOUGHING TEAM with an Overtime Tractor, outside the Bishop's Palace in May 1918. They won the championship for the greatest number of acres ploughed in one month – 154 acres, with a nine inch, three-furrow Cockshutt plough. From left to right: R.P. Ravenhill, Herbert 'Mickey' Minton (the champion cyclist and mechanic), S.M. Powell (ploughman), J.Wall (ploughman), A.R. Groom and E. Williams who supervised the organisation and supplies.

NAYLOR'S DIRECTORS AND EMPLOYEES pose for a record photograph in 1908. The founder of the firm, Mr T. Naylor, is seated in the front (in a deck chair) and his three sons are on either side and behind his chair.

PART OF THE MACHINE SHOP with lathes of all sizes and machines for punching, shearing, slotting, milling, grinding and facing, as well as the latest gear-cutting machinery.

INTERIOR OF THE OIL ENGINE ASSEMBLY SHOP showing oil engines from 2 bhp to 25 bhp in the course of construction.

THE INTERIOR OF THE MOTOR MANUFACTURING DEPARTMENT showing the switchboard for charging accumulators, the hollow spindle self-acting lathe and also a new car in the course of assembly. Naylors also made any type of agricultural machinery as well as oil engines and steam tractors.

THE STAFF OF JAMES FRYER'S GARAGE, Aubrey Street, c. 1910. Mr G.H. Butcher, Manager, is in the centre, on his right is Mr Corbett Winder. Archie Davies, seated on the extreme left, was the first on the staff and 50 years later he came back as a washer of cars! The car they are proudly surrounding is probably a Humber. Mr Butcher started the garage at the Green Dragon yard for James Fryer in 1908. The photograph was taken at the top of the yard before it was roofed over.

AN UNUSUAL VIEW OF THE WORKSHOP at the Aubrey Street Garage of James Fryer Ltd. in c. 1920. On the left is Mr B.C. Day, the Works Manager.

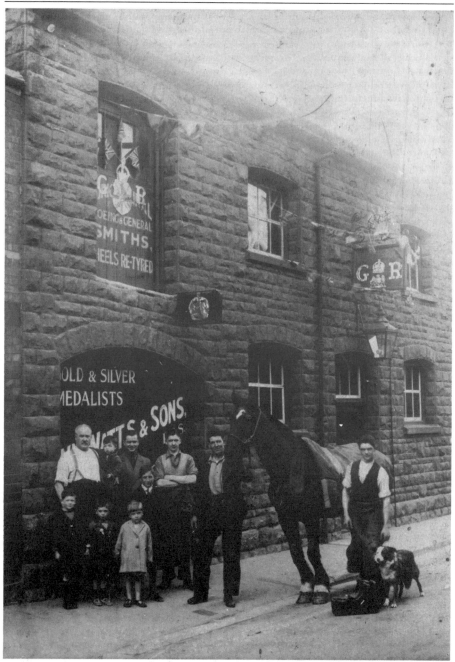

CORONATION BUNTING graces the famous premises of the Watts' family of blacksmiths in Blueschool Street.

MRS BARNETT at the doorway of her husband's renowned basket-makers workshop in Union Street, c. 1900. Repairs to all types of chairs were undertaken and every kind of plain, fancy, travelling, household and trade baskets were made on the premises and sold in the Market Hall. Their speciality was giant laundry baskets.

THE STAFF OF HATTON'S BOOT SHOP, St Peter's Street, c. 1870, holding the tools of the trade. The youngest member of staff is 11 years old.

THE STAFF OF MARSHALL AND WRIGHT, TAILORS, at the rear of their premises in Commercial Street, with tools and tapes of the trade, c. 1900.

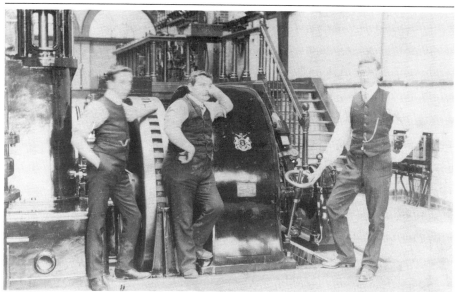

MESSRS A.J. MORRIS, W. PERKS AND H.E. MUNDAY posing in the engine room of Hereford City Electrics Works, opened in 1899, in Widemarsh Street. Electricity was daily used in Hereford for all the usual uses, such as lighting and heating, but also for chaff cutting, bottle washing, coffee grinding and even to heat flat irons! Electrical Exhibitions showing the many uses of electricity were held each year in the Shirehall.

A VIEW OF THE HEREFORD ELECTRICITY WORKS ENGINE ROOM. It had five steam-driven direct-coupled generators; a Triple Expansion Engine coupled to a multi-polar dynamo moving at a speed of 375 revs. per minute, a steam Balancer set at 100 hp, a Triple Expansion engine set at 500 hp and two compound steam engines of 175 hp. These ran at speeds of up to 900 revs. per minute and if necessary, they would run for weeks without a stop.

HEREFORD CITY POLICE, proudly posing in 1922. PC James, PC Price, PC Wall, PC Saunders, PC Penry, PC Johnson (Asst. Clerk), PC Preece; PC Bromage, PC Lewis, PC Arthur Morris, PC F. Davies, PC Cousins, PC Roberts, PC Everall, PC Dawe, PC Smith, PC Stephens, PC Harris, PC H. Davies, PC Stroud, PC Burgess, PC Spencer, PC Prosser, PC Albert Morris, PC Good, PC F. Bromage, PC Bird, PC Hirons; Det-Con. Hall, Sgt. Niblett, Sgt. Daffurn, Insp. Price, Coun. M.C. Oatfield J.P. (Mayor & Chairman of Watch Committee). Chief-Con. Rawson, Insp. Munn, Sgt. Edwards, Sgt. Hadley, Sgt. Wheatley DCM (Chief Clerk), Det-Insp. Hoskins.

ANOTHER FINE BODY OF MEN! The Hereford Fire Brigade in 1909. On the steam engine: driver – Fireman Elijah Bowers; standing, Firemen Charles Grisman, James Hales and Albert Jones; seated, Firemen Daniel O'Neale, Edwin Errington, Charles Beeks; on footplate of the engine, Chief Engineer Francis Smith. On the ground, Firemen Thomas Jones, John Husbands, Walter Hick, Lieut. John Beeks, Chief Officer Frank Richardson, Sub-Engineer George Daffwn, Firemen Alfred Gagg, Thomas Baird and Chief Waterman John Baird.

THE STAFF OF THE WORKHOUSE, now the County Hospital. The late Gilbert Harding's mother, the Matron, is seated, third from the left. The Workhouse was built in 1836 and was capable of accommodating 300 inmates.

A RARE PHOTOGRAPH OF SUFFRAGETTE ACTIVITY IN HEREFORD. Miss Lamond (centre) and her co-workers hold a meeting in the Suffrage Committee Room, St Peter's House, St Peter's Square in 1909.

YOUNG VOLUNTEERS 'muster' for military service, on Castle Green in 1914. The Nelson Monument, built in 1809, stands sentinel.

THE HEREFORDSHIRE REGIMENT VOLUNTEERS at Church Parade on Castle Green.

A SCHOOL GARDENING CLASS, c. 1940s, but where?

HOLMER SCHOOL c. 1916. Well washed and brushed pupils, but the back row look distinctly under duress!

THE BARTON GREAT WESTERN RAILWAY AMBULANCE TEAM, in 1908. They seem to be well prepared for anything! Left to right: J. Bencham (Loco-super), C. Kirk (Captain), W. Redding, C. Challoner, A. Hiron, A. James (patient). Kneeling: J. Lodge and G. Arrowsmith.

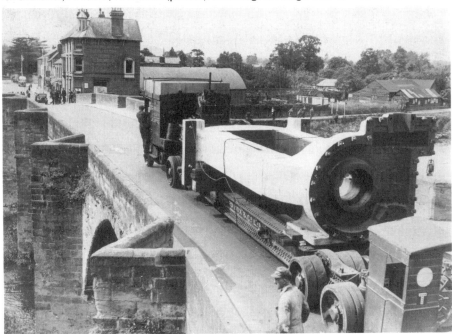

A HEAVY MILITARY LOAD crosses the Wye Bridge in March 1940. This contribution to the war effort got stuck – much to the consternation of Herefordians as all traffic stopped for some hours!

THE HEADQUARTERS STAFF OF THE HEREFORD HOME GUARD. Back row: Sigr. Moore, J.R.J., Sigr. Jones, C.L., Cpl. Binns, G.W., L./Cpl. Snell, H., Cpl. Rutherford, J., Sgt. Perks, E., Sigr. Wegg-Prosser, M.J., Sgt. Foltynier, R.J., Cpl. Palmer, A.J., Cpl. Godwin, H.J., Sgt. Simpson, C.W.T., Sigr. Reece, H.F., Sigr. Price, R.J., L/Cpl. Holloway, W.J. Middle row: L/Cpl. Pearce, M.J., Sgt. Hiles, J.J., Mrs J. Badham, Lieut. H.B.N. Morgan, Lieut. W.J. Gore, Capt. A.E. Holmes, Capt. W. Barnes, Lieut. R.A.S. Hill, Lieut. H.R.R. Jones, Miss B.G. Farr, Miss J.E. Meredith, S/Sgt. Mollison, W., Sgt. Warr, M.J. Front row: Major F.B. Hewitt (Loyals), Major C.W.R. Cann (R.A.), Capt. F. Lewis-Smith, Capt. P. Lamputt, Major J.V.S. Rutter, Lt-Col. G.W. Dryland, Col. H.G.F. Frisby (Comd.), Major K.G.S. Hatfield, Capt. H.J. Chapman, Capt. A. Haggard, Capt. C.A. Ireland, Major D.C. Robinson, M.C. (R.W.F.).

THE THIRD HEREFORDSHIRE (HEREFORD CITY) BATTALION HOME GUARD, 'D' Company spigot mortar team. Exercises took place on the Rugby ground, Wyeside.

THIRD HEREFORDSHIRE (HEREFORD CITY) BATTALION HOME GUARD, 'D' Company 6-Pounder Gun Team with Beaverette.

THE ROOF WATCHERS.
1142.

A HEREFORD MEMENTO OF THE 1939-45 WAR

1942.

A WARTIME POSTCARD showing keen-eyed fire watchers in Bridge Street, adjacent to large granaries, watching out for incendiary bombs and protecting the food reserves. The sketch depicts an imaginary view of Hereford Castle undergoing an attack 800 years before.

HEREFORD OCTOBER FAIR, a busy scene in the stock market in October 1910. Before the building of the Cattle Market in 1856 the Cattle Fair was held in Broad Street.

HAYMAKING ON THE LUGG MEADOWS on the outskirts of the city, c. 1900. The 'Hereford' wagon was very probably made in the city, possibly by Jones of Blueschool Street.

AN OPEN AIR MEETING OF HOP GROWERS in High Town in May 1908. The address is being given by Mr F. Pennefather.

WEDNESDAY AT HEREFORD FRUIT MARKET, October 1907. It was built in 1897 on the west side of the Cattle Market, under the management of Messrs. Meats & Meats.

HEREFORD BREWERY COOPERS' SHOP, Bewell Street, in 1880. All the barrels for the brewery were made and repaired here. Alfred Watkins' photograph captures well the busy atmosphere of this vital part of the brewery.

PENSIONERS AT CONINGSBY HOSPITAL, photographed by Alfred Watkins in 1890. They are chatting at the entrance to their refectory, now the fascinating St John Medieval Museum which depicts the lives of the pensioners in the seventeenth century, together with the history of the Knight Hospitallers of St John of Jerusalem.

A CORPORAL PENSIONER in the quadrangle at Coningsby Hospital in Widemarsh Street, in full uniform with the Coningsby Conies (Rabbits!) badge, c. 1910. A corporal was paid £20 per annum and was allowed to marry and live in one of the twelve almshouses. The modernised almshouses are still in use today.

DETECTIVE INSPECTOR OVENS investigating the recovery of over 2000 books in Hereford after a theft in May 1908. The Inspector had the task of checking all the titles!

Highdays and Holidays

A FORMAL DINNER IN THE TOWN HALL to celebrate the 95th Anniversary of the *Hereford Times* in 1927. Note the 'Ladies' Table' in the centre, presumably *Times* employees, with a rose floral arrangement, surrounded by the gentlemen with their vases of asters!

LEDBURY'S SON, the Poet Laureate John Masefield, D.Litt., Litt.D., LLD, receives the applewood box and scroll of Freedom of the City of Hereford in October 1930, from the Mayor, Mrs Luard.

THE HEREFORDSHIRE REGIMENT having received the Freedom of the City, march through St Peter's Square in September 1945. The Mayor, T. Powell, took the salute.

THE CITIZENS OF HEREFORD gather outside the Town Hall to hear the proclamation of King George V on 10 May 1910 by the Mayor, Walter Pilley.

WALTER PILLEY, the Mayor and the Corporation leave Hereford Roman Catholic Church, Broad Street, after a service in May 1910. He was the first Roman Catholic Mayor of Hereford for nearly 400 years and the first to attend a Catholic Service in his official capacity, in Hereford.

SOLEMN CELEBRATIONS take place at the Cathedral's West Front on 14 May 1907. The Earl of Warwick, as past Deputy Grand Master of England, is accompanied by Freemasons, Clergy and the Mayor and Corporation to lay the cornerstone of the Masonic turret in the new West Front.

SIR JAMES RANKIN receiving an enthusiastic reception when addressing his supporters at the Mitre Hotel, Broad Street, after the Parliamentary Election of February 1910.

THE HEREFORDSHIRE REGIMENT marching through the city. The exact date is not known, but it is possibly an Empire Day between the Wars.

HIGH TOWN, 13 May 1902, on the occasion of the visit of the Princess Henry of Battenberg to the city. She had a very hectic round of engagements, investing the foundation stone of the Town Hall, attending the Cathedral service to unveil a window in honour of her mother, Queen Victoria and finally here presenting medals to Boer War soldiers, watched by what appears to be the whole city!

EAGER CHILDREN are marshalled on Aylestone Hill near the station for a glimpse of the Royal train bringing King Edward VII and Queen Alexandra to Hereford in July 1908.

VISITING HEREFORD on 24 April 1957, the Queen is welcomed by the Mayor, C.J. Gooding, and Mayoress at the Town Hall.

JUBILEE CELEBRATION, Castle Green, 1897. All the local schools sent groups to dance around the Maypole and gave exhibitions of country dancing. May Day was always a big social occasion in Hereford, a chance to show off a new spring outfit and hat! A Maypole stood in High Town until the beginning of the nineteenth century when it was erected on Castle Green.

MESSRS HEINS & CO.'S GRAMOPHONE CONCERT on Castle Green, in glorious weather, September 1908.

THE HIGH TOWN PROCESSION, before the launch of the lifeboat onto the river.

LIFEBOAT LAUNCH on the river to celebrate Lifeboat Saturday, October 1908, from Castle Green.

THE TWENTIETH CENTURY FRIENDLY SOCIETY'S TABLEAU on show during Lifeboat Saturday in Hereford, October 1908.

THE WINNERS OF THE LIFEBOAT SATURDAY CARNIVAL COMPETITION. Left, Mr E.W. Longford's illuminated motor car. Right, the cyclist entries: Miss Morrish, first prizewinner, is in the centre.

HEREFORD CITY AND COUNTY CONSTITUTIONAL WHIST DRIVE in the Town Hall in June 1911. Mr Arkwright MP presented the prizes to the winners amongst the 350 present.

MR E. STANTON JONES' BAND appearing in Hereford for the last time as the Herefordshire Battalion Band, in September 1908.

HEREFORD SALVATION ARMY. Christmas treat preparations in January 1911 for over 400 poor children. Adjutant and Mrs Young are in the back row on the right.

VE DAY, 1945 in Hawthorn Grove, Hinton. This fine street party shows the young Cratchley family on the right, Jean, Tony and Maureen. Many street parties took place, but this superb photograph is the only one available to show the joy and excitement of all Herefordians.

A 'NOVEL' FLORAL DISPLAY exhibited by Kings Acre Nurseries at the Hereford Fruit & Chrysanthemum Society's Show in the Shirehall in 1908. The swans were made of roses and white chrysanthemums, with lily petals for wings.

A FINE DISPLAY OF 'CRANSTON EXCELSIOR' ONIONS at Wilson's Horticultural Show at Hereford in September 1910.

THE WOOLHOPE NATURALIST FIELD CLUB CENTENARY PHOTOGRAPH taken near Dormington Wood, 23 June 1951. Many well-known faces can be seen in this photograph including F.C. Morgan and Gavin Robinson. The Woolhope Club's Room and Library are still in the City Museum, originally built in 1874 to house their collections.

VISITORS TO THE 1897 THREE CHOIRS FESTIVAL walk to their carriage rank in Broad Street, watched over by a beat Constable. Hereford always welcomed visitors from far and wide, as it does today, to this, the oldest Music Festival in Europe.

SIR EDWARD ELGAR outside the cathedral at the Three Choirs Festival in 1933. From left to right: H.K. Foster (Secretary of Festival), Dr Percy Hull (Hereford), Sir Edward Elgar, Sir Ivor Atkins (Worcester) and H.W. Sumsian (Gloucester).

THE FULL CHOIR AND ORCHESTRA in Hereford Cathedral during the Three Choirs Music Festival, 1958, held in turn in the cathedral cities of Worcester, Gloucester and Hereford.

THE THREE CHOIRS CHORISTERS in full voice in Hereford, 1958.

BENJAMIN BRITTEN AND PETER PEARS meet a group of schoolgirls from Ross-on-Wye High School Girls' Choir, outside the west door of Hereford Cathedral in 1961.

A WELCOME ARCH built across Broad Street for the Three Choirs Festival, 1908. The Festival was visited by Princess May and the Duke of York, later their Majesties Queen Mary and George V. The arch artistically represents the Victoria Bridge and was built by W.K. Goodall and the staff of Samuel Searle, Furnishers, of Widemarsh Street. Mr Goodall, in the straw hat, can be seen on the arch admiring his design.

THE WONDERFUL STEAM GALLOPERS of Studt's 'Grand Steeplechase' in High Town, in the 1907 May Fair.

THE SPRAWL OF HEREFORD'S MAY FAIR in High Town, 1884.

THE LADY DANCERS in Dutch girl costumes at Studt's Show in Hereford May Fair, 1907.

Disaster, Fire and Flood

THE CATHEDRAL CLOSE GATES AND BUILDING fronting the Close in September 1934, which includes Ellis the Saddler.

THE HOUSES IN FRONT OF THE CATHEDRAL CLOSE, in Broad Street, on fire, 29 April 1935.

DEMOLITION COMMENCES 21 May 1935. The cathedral can now be seen from Broad Street, for the first time for over 100 years.

THE LAST WALL FALLS and the cathedral is fully revealed.

AN EXTRAORDINARY ACCIDENT in High Town in 1910. The scene at Messrs Greenlands Ltd., showing the window (marked X) through which a runaway horse, ridden by Mr Thomas Wood of Thruxton Court, rushed through, carrying with it and seriously injuring Mrs Elizabeth Barber of 3 Brecon Road, Hay. Willie Lewis, aged 15 of Portfield Street, was also struck by the horse and several others experienced a narrow escape. The window was 'smashed to atoms', as the *Hereford Times* eagerly reported!

In Ever Loving Remembrance

of

Nellie Rutherford.   Peggy Baird.   Cissie Beavan.   Violet Corey.

Winnie Mailes.   Linda Illman.   Phyllis White.   Connie Bragg.

Who passed into fuller and richer life on Friday, April 7th, 1916, in the performance of a public duty.

God keep the little children,
Whom we no more shall see;
Fled from their nests, and gone to rest,
Where we desire to be.

" One touch of nature makes the whole world akin."

A SAD CHAPTER IN THE LIFE OF THE CITY. These eight little girls were taking part in a concert at the Garrick Theatre to aid the Troops when their cotton wool costumes caught fire. The Mayor, G.B. Greenland, opened a fund to raise £500 to endow a cot in the children's ward at The Herefordshire General Hospital in their memory. The response was quick and generous.

THE SOUTH END OF THE WYE BRIDGE, the river in flood at 13ft. in 1928. No need of H. Chesterman's services!

THE 'TREMENDOUS FLOOD' of January 1899.

HEAVY, 16 FOOT FLOODS in December 1910, taken near the Saracen's Head.

THE FLOODS IN ST MARTIN'S STREET, 1947. The houses in the background were pulled down to make way for the roundabout. The houses on the right were pulled down for the approach to the new Greyfriars Bridge and petrol depot. Immediately behind the beleagured lorry is the Watts and Boelt's Bakery.

TWO SMALL BOYS EXPLORE FLOOD POOLS during the bad flooding of 27 August 1912.

BREAKING THE ICE. A stereoscopic photograph taken on 8 February 1895.

SECTION SIX

Recreation

A DELIGHTFUL VIEW OF THE CITY through the Hunderton Railway Bridge late on an idyllic Edwardian summer day.

A WONDERFULLY EVOCATIVE PHOTOGRAPH OF CHILDHOOD; a small group playing near the Victoria Bridge c. 1899. Fishing with a stick and jar still takes place on the riverbank, but one does not see such a fine yacht sailing today.

THE IMPRESSIVE STEPS OF HEREFORD ROWING CLUB, Greyfriars Avenue, in c. 1900. The boathouse was built in 1888. The Annual Regatta was held on the third Saturday in July, but now is on the Spring Bank Holiday. The Rowing Club is still an important feature of sporting life in the city.

THE FLOODED WYE BRIDGE, 25 July 1894.

JORDAN'S BOATHOUSE AND BOATS stranded by the 13ft. flood of 1894. The children, plus dog, are waiting for the boats to be swept away!

'THE FURRIER OF THE WEST'. Gus Edwards standing by his boat below the old netting hut and gear, 17 May 1893.

HEREFORD REGATTA c. 1900. Note the Marshals and Judges on the right-hand bank.

MR & MRS ALFRED WATKINS at Hereford Regatta c. 1900. Alfred Watkins, famous photographer, inventor, antiquarian and author of *The Old Straight Track*, rarely captured on film at such a relaxed social occasion.

PARKER'S STEAMER at Belmont on 2 July 1894, with members of the Hatton family taking tea by the riverbank and even enjoying a paddle on this glorious summer day.

THE UNUSUAL SIGHT OF A YACHT on the River Wye, c. 1895, reputed to be the last such craft built on the Wye.

THE OPENING OF THE NEW BATHING PAVILION at Bartonsham, July 1910.

CECIL GETHEN'S SPLENDID PHOTOGRAPH OF THE FROZEN RIVER WYE on 30 December 1892, depicts the Victorian delight in skating. Many Herefordians had skates and used them most winters on the river from Jordan's boatyard to Hunderton; at times there were 600 skaters on the ice at once. The other skating centre was the Castle Pool, where a series of moonlit 'Ice Carnivals' were arranged by Mr Wilson the Green Keeper, to raise money for needy families to obtain fuel.

THE FROZEN RIVER WYE in 1895.

QUEEN VICTORIA'S JUBILEE SPORTS held in Edgar Street, 1897.

ST OWENS AND BLUE COAT SCHOOL CRICKET XI 1928. J. Sawyer, 'W.W.W.', J. Jay, J. Morgan, D. Preece, Mr Morgen, J. Silvester, (Capt.), Mr Meyrick, A. Everard, G. Almrott, S. Williams, R. Richards.

A WONDERFUL ARRAY OF CHARACTERS at a Fancy Dress Carnival at Hereford Roller-Skating Rink in March 1911.

THE 'TOP HATS' V 'THE BONNETS', rival football teams accompanied by the Referee 'Long Jim' in the charge of Mr W.E.J. Roberts. When and where?

EVANS FOOTBALL CLUB, 1935–6.

LADIES ARCHERY ROUND MEETING in September 1908. Top row, left to right: Miss Carr, Miss E. Harkness, Miss Laing, Miss Price, Miss Fixson, Miss Newall, Mrs Hill-Lowe, Mrs Lewis, Miss Ruxton, Miss Bridgford, Mrs Sandford. Middle row: Mr Battiscombe (Judge), Mrs W. Aubrey, Miss Rushton, Miss Tat Thomas, Mrs Leonard, Miss Harkness, Mrs Day, Miss Hyne, Miss Bethell, Miss Phillips, Miss Bird, Mrs Battiscombe. Front row: Mrs Appleford, Miss Thackwell, Mrs Wadsworth, Mrs Armitage, Miss Hussey, Mrs Rushton, Miss Wright, S.H. Armitage (Hon. Sec.). The Hon. Secretary looks suitably dwarfed by the formidable group of skilled and lethal ladies!

SUITABLY ATTIRED, Harry Price attempts to mount his bicycle on 2 October 1893.

THE HEREFORD ROAD CYCLING CLUB takes a rest in June 1908. The cars were to carry refreshments! The blue Humberette, CJ 85, was registered on 1 January 1904.

HERBERT (MICKEY) MINTON, the champion Hereford cyclist. As an amateur he achieved two World Records, 4 NCU Championships, won numerous cups and acquired 200 first, 140 second and 80 third prizes.

THE HOLMER SCHOOL SWIMMING TEAM who won the Hereford Schools' Swimming Challenge Shield in January 1911. The shield was presented at the Town Hall by Mr Bulmer, deputy Mayor. The team included W. Walker, W. Grubb, W. Mace and T.W. Wilkins, watched by the proud headmaster, D.W. Harris (right) and H.E. Pile, second master, on the left.

FANCY DRESS SOCIAL AND DANCE at the Swimming Baths, Kyrle Street, in 1911. The baths were built by the Hereford Industrial Aid Society and had male and female attendants. The female attendants had to be married!

A FINE BODY OF MEN IN THE HEREFORD GYMNASIUM CLUB in 1908. First row: A. Chanty, W.H. Taylor, A. Stephens, J.T. James and W. Connell. Second row: W. Griffiths, P. Delves, J. Higginson, E.S. Richards, T. Robbins, and S.G. Sherer. Third row: E.A. Garnett, A. Berry (sec.), H.J. Lawrence, P. Thomas (instructor), Geo. Vale, H.H. Illman and W. Thomas. Fourth row: A.E. Silkston and W.A. Smith.

HEREFORD HOCKEY CLUB at Edgar Street, January 1911.

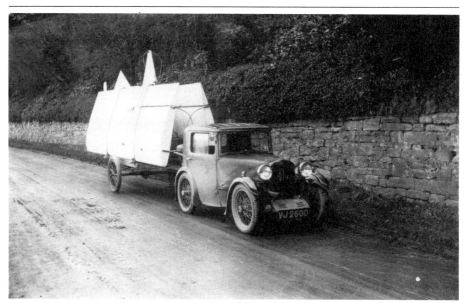

MR PERCY PRITCHARD'S MG towing a glider in 1930 from Hereford to a meeting of the South Shropshire and North Herefordshire Gliding Club.

WALTER PRITCHARD'S PHOTOGRAPH OF A GLIDER with Percy Pritchard at the controls, ready for the word . . . 'release'! The South Shropshire and North Herefordshire Gliding Club enthusiasts often met at Dinmore for 'motorless flying'.

THE POST OFFICE RIFLE CLUB in 1910. The committee and team which shot in the Matthew Nathan Cup Competition in June. Back row left to right: D.J. Beard, W. Michael, E.J. Moore, W. Bowen, H.A. Sheffield, G.J. Haynes, W.C. Grisman (range attendant). Second row seated: P. Wedge, C. Jones, O. Bromfield. Front row: R.T. Palmer, C.J. Baynham and H. Prosser.

HOMING PIGEONS at Barrs Court Station, 1907. To the left, the baskets have arrived safely. To the right, the birds are being released by the conveyor, Mr W.F. Lawrence. Many birds from Herefordshire flew back from the Channel Islands and France in competitions.

'THE OLD CRICKET GROUND', as it was called, on Widemarsh Common in December 1908. The half-timbering is rather attractive! Hereford Cricket Club was first established here in 1836.

THE DECEMBER MIST in 1908, almost obscures the staff preparing the new Cricket Ground in front of the grandstand on the racecourse. On completion, the County Club moved its HQ here in 1909 and the City Corporation purchased its pavilion.

THE COUNTIES CHESS ASSOCIATION MASTERS TOURNAMENT, Hereford, August 1885.

Opposite, lower picture:
THE FINE ART DECO INTERIOR of Oscar Deutch's Hereford Odeon, 'Home of British Pictures'. The plush 'Sandringham' seats by Turner had just been bolted into position. It is interesting to note that the Bush Thompson-Houston sound equipment had built-in deaf-aids. The decor was personally designed by Mrs Oscar Deutch, no two theatres being exactly alike. Founded in 1933, The Odeon Organisation had over 50 cinemas under construction when Hereford's example opened in 1937 – how many are left today? One of the clocks in the photograph was rescued by the City Museums during demolition and is in public use again for the benefit of staff and visitors!

THE SPLENDID ODEON THEATRE at its grand opening on 17 April 1937. Designed by Roland Sutwell, the contractors were W.H. Peake & Sons of Barton Works, Hereford. The Mayor, Mrs Luard MBE, graciously opened the Odeon and the Band of the Scots Guards played the musical interlude before the Gaumont British News; a cartoon and then the main feature, starring Will Hay, followed.

THE ODEON, COMMERCIAL STREET, in its opening 1930s splendour. Very familiar to generations of Herefordians it is no more, because it was recently demolished to facilitate the building of the Maylord Orchards Development.

Castle Green and Nelson Monument.   *Hereford.*

A DELIGHTFUL VIEW OF THE CASTLE GREEN AND THE NELSON MONUMENT on this postcard of c. 1904, with the Art School on the left of the picture. Two of the cannon at the base of the monument are in Churchill Gardens, as is 'Roaring Meg' the Civil War mortar, but there are reputed to have been other cannon at one time. The card is written to a Miss Richards and is not signed, but the message is 'I'll tell your Mother, going to Church with that Bryn on Sunday'!

THE TRANQUIL RIVER WYE taken from the Wye Bridge c. 1912, with Jordan's pleasure boats on the left.

'REFLECTIONS ... ! 1900.

SECTION SEVEN

Transport

THE FAMOUS NELL GWYNNE FIRE ENGINE in steam, shortly after its delivery from the Sandringham estate. Purchased in 1880, it was sadly sold in 1927. The City does still possess a manual fire engine which is on loan to the Waterworks Museum, Broomy Hill, Hereford.

THE HORSE-DRAWN MERRYWEATHER MANUAL FIRE ENGINE AND HOSE CART in Hereford Fire Station, Gaol Street, in 1892.

MEMBERS OF THE TOWNSEND FAMILY outside the Golden Cross, 9 Maylord Street, in their fine vehicle, (a Wolsley?)

Overleaf:
PRINCE HENRY OF PRUSSIA (brother of the Kaiser) in his Benz, during a visit by the German Automobile Club to Hereford, waiting outside the Mitre Hotel in Broad Street, 18 July 1911. The Prince stopped for lunch and was enthusiastically greeted by Herefordians, some of whom can be identified – the man in the bowler behind the car hood is Mr Sessarego the jeweller, the lady in white with the flag is Miss Maud Bull. Inspector Ovens, W.W. Robinson the architect, Mr Cockcroft the librarian and Mr Palmer the postman, can also be seen watching the spectacle.

THIS FINE SHOOTING BRAKE of c. 1910, belonged to the Earl of Lonsdale and was used as an advert for the longevity of Commer cars. It was sent to all the Commer distributors including James Fryer Ltd. in Widemarsh Street, where the publicity photograph was taken in c. 1935.

THE
GREEN DRAGON HOTEL
COMPANY,
HEREFORD,
(LIMITED),

Invite attention to the above House, which has recently been greatly enlarged,
for the reception of Families and Commercial Gentlemen.

THE HOUSE WILL BE FOUND REPLETE WITH EVERY COMFORT,

AND THE

𝔚ines of the 𝔅est 𝔔uality.

A SEPARATE COFFEE ROOM FOR LADIES.

HOT AND COLD BATHS.

THE CHARGE FOR ATTENDANCE IS INCLUDED IN THE BILLS.

OMNIBUSES TO AND FROM EVERY TRAIN.

ELLEN JERMYN, Manager.

1863 advertisement – see pages 22 and 23.

MOTOR COACH TOURS

THE

HEREFORD MOTOR CO., LTD.,

Will run DAILY TOURS (except Sundays) to the following
places, subject to sufficient passengers being available and
circumstances permitting —

MALVERN

SYMOND'S YAT

CHEPSTOW

TINTERN

ROSS

MONMOUTH

LUDLOW

For particulars of Daily Tours see small bills. Passengers are
invited to Book their Seats in Advance at the Offices:

ST. GEORGE'S GARAGE, EIGN STREET,

where Seating Plan can be seen

PRIVATE OPEN AND CLOSED CARS FOR HIRE.

1920s advertisement.

LARGE GARAGE.   REPAIRS.

Phone 1174

151

THE WINNING MOTOR CARS AND THEIR DRIVERS from the Fromes Hill Trials in April 1908. Messrs Naylor & Co. Ltd. of Friar Street, Hereford, were also appointed by the Royal Automobile Club, in 1906 and 1907, to officially gauge the victorious cars.

TWO FINE EARLY MORGAN THREE-WHEELERS in the 1913 Hereford Small Car Trials, much admired by the Eton-collared boy spectators.

GURNEY'S SUPERB FLEET OF MOTOR VANS in Commercial Road in 1908. Founded in 1858 by Alfred Gurney, this family grocers and wine merchants was well-known in the city and county. It was one of the first firms in the city to use motor vans.

MR CHUBB ON HIS MINERVA MOTOR CYCLE, beside the Whitecross, in 1903. This bicycle was registered as CJ 28 on 1 January 1904. The motor bike still exists, in a fully restored condition, in a private collection.

MISS TOWNSEND with her new bicycle from Townsend's shop at 24 High Town, c. 1890.

MR FRANK TITTERTON AND CHAUFFEUR with his new Standard 12 outside Hereford Cathedral and opposite Palace yard in 1933. The building to the left in the Close was demolished, as was the 'Residence' in the background, next door to the City Museum & Library.

'ABERDARE', during the First World War, hauling a goods train, (armaments?), over Hunderton bridge.

A LOCOMOTIVE overturned on the turntable at Barton Station, C. 1900.

THE LONDON & NORTH-WESTERN RAILWAY COMPANY DRAYMEN AND HORSES at Barrs Court in November 1909.

THE CASTLE GREEN FERRY before the Victoria Bridge was built in 1897. Note the *Princess May* ferry boat by the far bank and the ferryman's hut that somewhat resembled a guardsman's sentry box!

A POLICEMAN'S LOT…! A winter's day in 1893.

TRANQUIL VIEW OF HEREFORD INFIRMARY by the river on 17 May 1893.

ACKNOWLEDGEMENTS

I welcome this opportunity to express my thanks to the many who have assisted me in the compilation of this book and for the sharing of their knowledge; Hereford City Library (Mr B.J. Whitehouse and his staff) and Hereford City Council, for the use of the many photographs from their respective collections. Similarly I am extremely grateful for advice and the loan of material from Mr B. Butcher, Mr P. Pritchard ARPS, Miss Jenner, Mrs J. Goode, Mr E. Hatton, Mr E. Bettington, Miss J. Wilson and Mr D. Foxton.

Every effort has been made to ascertain photographic copyright where appropriate.

Very special thanks are due to Eve Finney, Ken Hoverd, Derek Evans and Richard Hammonds and finally my husband, David Berry, for all his help and encouragement.